UNDER NEW ALCHEMY

DEREK FENNER

FIRST EDITION

MILLS RIVER, NC

BOOTSTRAP PRESS

2025

Art is Love is God.

–Wallace Berman

ISBN 13: 978-1-946741-16-5

Cover artwork by the author.

Author acknowledgements: I would like to thank every editor who welcomed my poems, especially Nicholas James Whittington, who gave life to *Gossamer Nevele Grimoire,* as well as Micah Ballard and Sunnylyn Thibodeaux for their summoning and printing of *Wild Schemes*—both reprinted in this book, and are beautiful manifestations of craft and care. I am equally indebted to my poetry comrades, whose insights have shaped these poems and this book—too many to name—but with a special nod to Nicholas James Whittington, Jason Morris, and Ryan Gallagher.

Bootsrap Press
Lowell, MA & Mills River, NC

www.bootstrappress.org

For my son, Oliver

Oh, carriers of murderous stars
Do not laugh at my agrarian gods
Because they have not broken the bridges
With the first salt of the earth: Man!

—Réne Depestre

I'm going to strip some of the last veils off right now.

And I'll be the one
to take care of the wounds.

—Roque Dalton

To go in the dark with a light is to know the light.
To know the dark, go dark. Go without sight,
and find that the dark, too, blooms and sings,
and is traveled by dark feet and dark wings.

—Wendell Berry

hero crack s human volume magic against time speak ing the strange science beneath wisdom

UNDER NEW ALCHEMY

When I thought
the ground beneath me
was solid & it moved
on with a different gravity
my stars aligned
with false alarms

Somewhere between
things promised
& reality—a wonderful
lushness overtook me
asked me to collect love
where it was taken

When I say infinity I mean now
with nothing left
to burn or sustain
I walk down the ground
      because in a landscape
      of scars
            nothing moves

VARIATIONS ON THE MARCH

Everybody is psychic
right before they die

I stop & listen to the street's
tone—a cascading drift

of language bangs
overhead carrier doves

spit on modern tombstones
condominiums in the kill zone

to incite a toppling cycle
I spread corn oil & wine

over new cornerstones
over these landmarks

of eternal occupation
it's starting to feel

like fatality has its comforts
in sleeping I go nowhere

looking like a corpse
that has accepted its rest

on the way to the march
I pass new recruits

expecting humiliation
as they are mocked

trampled & speaking
in bankers' tongues

a narrow blade falls
from my hands

the wind mixed with vinegar
I am tripping over boxes

from old world wars
filled with receipts

from giant Detroit land grabs
red tape & the usual

gimmicks of liberalism
power won't leave

a state-won dystopia
it's been a year

of Eric Dolphy
or Black Sabbath

opaque isolation
while I text myself

cutting into already
salted wounds

a revolution of the stars
doesn't do anything

on the street
they are cultivating

divination in data dumps
& closing pool halls

for yoga & charter schools
green lighting coal money

& bike shares for upper
middle Citibank patrons

it has always been this bleak
it has always been this blank

collectively we remember imperialism
putting the rest on permanent mute

TOWER THROWING SHADE ON THE FALL

Ohio River Bridge
                    & buzzing pockets

Normalizing empire
                    is the way to empire
                    my heart is grass gravel & nothing solid

This multivarient reading
                    of the tree of life
                    McNaughton's
                    call upon the emptiness of all powers

The complaints
                    of the privileged
                    sitting there
                    taking up all that air

So in desperate afternoons
                    surveillance is downloaded
                    & held vigilant
                    in clandestine staring contests
                    minus traditional black mirrors

Sold minds stay in stasis
                    until we throw
                    sitting bankers
                    off chartered planes

The medicine is making us sick
                    ironic bartenders
                    serve sacred
                    cosmic promises
                    as pharmacological hoaxes
                    form the marine layer

Loan officers—

      modern vampires
      performing financial hexes
      saturating the masses
      in rent addiction
      & degenerate optimism

Everyday delirium

      through trance-actions
      uploading noisy mindless storms
      in digital flagellation

A Rosetta Stone of nothing but sound
      is getting permanent
      this holding on
      to the edge
      of the world

As a moniker whips by

      sinking birds of paradise
      be careful with those ice hooks—
      our luckiest scabs
      circulate empty deaths

Horizontal life itself

      enticed by hokey hope
      scrubbed of reason
      & knives on greasy sheets—
      the constant pressure
      of our own decay

This version of demonology is also the cure
      mirror-rapture has its loopholes
      & every plague
      its theory
      as graves open
      to glittery markets

I always looked forward
                    to being a mad scientist
                    but the funding was terrible
                    so I watched them institute
                    a program for the speaking

Every diary is a prison diary
                    we gleam obscene in the light

Dear Simulacra
                    we like to watch
                    our planet get dim—
                    settler colonialism
                    is the pre-existing condition

Trauma recorded as playlists—
                    all stations
                    divisible
                    by carceral panoptics
                    & data sharecropping

Complicit in my own cognitive sabotage
                    I busy myself with melancholy
                    avoiding occasions to connect

There are things we cannot stream
                    & so tonight
                    I return library books
                    with missing pages
                    to avoid my own
                    aesthetic exorcism

We must stop adulting oppression
                    onto our young
                    & all those *laid up in heaven*

We do not have an optics problem
                    we lack solidarity beyond empathy

CERTAIN MOVEMENTS AT GIVEN MOMENTS

Far too many humans in this beyond
The moon dies whenever we look
You make me foolish over & over
Twenty more times in torn deforested forests
Stupidity in my rising sign
A theatrics of pyrotechnics
No dancing among falling statues
Passing from one sovereign to the next acceleration
Bucky Fuller's spaceship disastrously veering off course
A shady time-imprint of knotted cane & Toledo sword
How will we ever replace every language we've submerged?
Not with some rando crystal
Scattering enriched guts of strangled rocks
& deny us then—persistent weather
We continue naming things that already had names
Durer's selfie in a coat with fur collar
Rrose Sélavy memeing
The commons was six kinds of magic
We have always been untrue in our unfriendly games

THE STORY OF THE SUN THAT DIED
YESTERDAY & HOW EVERYTHING'S DEAD
UNTIL THEN

Our bodies
ornaments
for banks
crashing
in streets
dreaming
of the mental
refreshment
of political ether

A life congested
with police
internally
& cops
externally

News headlines
that read
THE SMILING
REIGN OF
BUREAUCRATS
or WASPS
FLOCK WHERE
ORCHIDS BLOOM

One more step
in any direction
& I will be
fully possessed
with capital's
Rip Van Winkle

Displacement is
now the second
definition of
of "disaster"
after whiteness
in the expanding
bone dictionary
of Empire & we
are our crisis

The need to recognize
through hundreds of
years of oppression analysis
— that nothing
is different

We frame selfies
in nihilistic
museums
as the planet
returns to dust
& the moon
brushes
its shoulders off
in perpetuity

A tremendous ooze
escapes city hall
#vapelife is not
the revolution I was
waiting on

The altars
are too crowded
for actual healing
There's no room
for trees or people
in a city dedicated
to bandwidth

I look to crows
& how they
refuse migration—
watching the paling
of everything

Who will guard
the guards themselves

POISONOUS INGENUITY

In the shifting foundations of shaking houses
before the law "keeps itself kept by a doorkeeper
who keeps nothing, the door remaining open
& open onto nothing." Forget Derrida!
An electric vehicle for phantoms, the starlit meerkats—
a massive army of loving refusals.
The decadents have moved to the corner store
& there too slurpee death postures.
Under sun chip sabbaths a robbing gentrification
aka the creative economy expanding the western threshold.
Wrapped in sovereign body / sacred body
we cannot live forever in a city of men
exposed to death in the camera lens—
no longer living animals.
Our living cities will kill us all.

We hide with plastic lights all that really hangs above.

We float away in the city-distance.

We carry the past in pill-form.

We pray to the false promise of collapsing saints.

We abate a dimming big dipper.

We encourage the heart attack
     engaging the dominant distillation.

VOLUNTARY MEMORY

To confirm our fears
but even the chipping
is apt to raise
us in enormous open buildings

Roof connected to earth
a formative long beauty
under the fallen branch of dark

The green angel
takes her second helping
a stretched reply
on the narrow path
down the cliff

A vehicle for action
           all of us
                  petrified stones

We have reached the scale
           of no return
                  advertising as raiment

Unwanted screen grabs
           left to survive
                  half-lit memory

The primitive power we have
           to adjust our eyes
                  in precarious dilation

SOURCES OF THE MISCONCEPTION

We should
quit our jobs
in the light
of ending all things
in this constant dissection
of a giant's causeway
beneath these pages
a collapsing sun
& despite the locus(t)
nobody knows
we live many times
under two eternities
in a race with each other
& a tearing manifestation of
an organ playing
in arrested space
exceeding the functionality
of a dirty chalkboard cleaned
another paradox
of abandoned principles
drawing the day
everything crumbles
the future body sideways
a symbol skewed
clumsy & lame
scratched by the punch line
& those old feelings
so let's go until the alchemist
rises from the dimestore
between truth-telling
& exorcism
modernism is a war crime
that has to be resisted everywhere

KNOW MORE HEROES
For Ryan Gallagher

Let's drink mint juleps
to soften the nightmares
of reason & to the existence
of our modern saints

Weirdness runs deep today
& I dream by committee
in hollowed out cigar-boxes
filled with oils & painting knives

The rest is exploding behind drawn blinds
near Kennedy's Butter & Eggs as I
lose my connection to civilization
when I trivialize nonsense as routine

Deep shit tends to sweeten dreams
& all cosmologies turn
to protocols handed out
in group-text interrogation

In the alienation shorthand
of a polis without politics
it's easy to calm the storm
when you keep moving

Any chance to distance
imagination long enough
to make it new—no path
for modesty in nature...just hum

BY THEIR MAINTENANCE

No one left here
        to alarm us.   So
I close my eyes
        every day.
The first horse to win
        the Kentucky Derby was Aristides—
a long stride in 1875
        circling antiquity.
Winds were in agreement
        a swirl of roses   mint
& the jockey's breath
        held a whiff of coriander.
Smiling Rada gods all over
        the Southern United States—
there's always someone around you
        in exaltation   in living prayer.
"Serving sacrifice   crossing customs
        anticipating mail."
We are held in straightaways
        the blood—called red mercury—
a great solvent to erase a thousand dreams
        & the alchemist always imagines innocence
midway upon the journey of his life.
        Projected flat images are raised
to receive the supplication of fading
        starlight. Splendor Solis
denotes Harry Crosby's daring
        impossibility—threefold.
A surface exfoliated with pine sap
        suffers the delusion of stubborn text
breaks the ego's burnt skin
        & typesets melancholia.
If nothing is true how is it
        that borders follow migrants—
how is it that laws predict oppression?
        Please put down your hands—I see you

haunting ample benedictions in unison.
    Let me hold the gaze for a second
on those waves that break & do not—
    on the scattered ghosts of your intentions
all our lips growing round.
    Building passage in flight
leather-wrapped turkey feathers
    spreading the bruised burnt past
over our bodies & ashes ashes
    not a single blade of grass.
A selenite lunar talisman
    suspended from silver thread
just every star hanging
    in language compost.
In arranged chordal sounds
    the vibrating will of
one big retina drop.
    Orpheus & the lifting veil
waving avenues in the wake.
    A circus where Hermes passes
between the tangible transparent
    our hustle the shifting
elements of living things
    & so we nourish our spirit
a few shots of Reposado
    the call of the immortal
& a quick zipline to the basement
    of the Tenderloin.   Teen
witches greeting the poems—
    the snap of Banquet Tall Boys
& the crunch of peanuts carry us
    the snap of half a block
to a late dinner at Patrick & Ava's.
    That Whitman poem you read
still sticking to my ribs
    purifying the upside
of anxiety in a home where psychic
    functioning orients a labyrinth
of possibility through ALL talk—

a dissipating of the utilitarian
pressures of life.

Some bourbon undulation
    against the radiating splendor
of Jack London dive bars
    concealing horror show
in sublime visions of voice.
    A timing gone & we are quick
to trample love in the race
    for capital desires.
As to I as magic
    is to mysticism devouring
defiance. At one soft-lit
    corner I read sun-damaged books
always a dude next to me
    wants to know what's inside—
a manuscript missing grids
    the double-loop of the zodiac
until he's back to covering his bets
    leaving me to the mystery of letters.
There's something nice
    about a dark little community
but sever the internet
    jukebox & favor Harvey's
Bristol Cream at Land's End.
    9 AM somewhere Seger is on—
we attempt poker without cards
    a game of evening divination.
How every May new ink marks
    landscape's memory on this body
but the second time Adderall
    kicks in is the last time
we feel anything without rubbing
    goofer dust on our wounds.
Idle to believe it is not possible
    with incense & Paul Masson
threatened by the Figures hereafter
    & the planetary intelligence of tea—

the apothecary in the forever
    of a photograph of Scorpio
in the 9th house film return.
    4 million fluttering pulses
& online is dead because
    every moment there
a license to depart.
    Side B
the poet
    at sea
fingernails
    the Titanic.
We walk the cursing light
    of dropping eyes
in the emptiness
    of Hop-On Hop-Off buses
or the window plants at Vesuvios.
    In the stammer their maintenance
amok & monstrous in the memory
    of Iroquois world identity.
An account is a given translation
    translateral rides into the sun.
What we put butterflies through—
    Migration should be marked
shifting radiance.

In fire somebody dangles a key
    Ritual is for when
you don't know what to do.
    Dada / Yaqui / Hero / Lil
raised by dawn & written
    at its countertop.
That was a heck of a hit
    upon the tape of time
that Meltzer nabbed
    & lets it go at that—
each eye down by the sea
    watching the man electric
even Kabalah-like awkward awesome

switches to singing
from the mutilated Ecco Homo
    to the Deleuzian body
without an organ-player
    swinging low bearing skin
in exchange for windy initiations.
    The crossroads are smoking
with offerings.
    The places we stood
under willow trees
    under magnolia
imaginary shrapnel
    & the Tempest in Lacan.
Never trade selva oscura
    for a world of sleepy monsters
for image-tyranny with your
    saint stripped up over the eye.
Everyday somebody paints by
    accident the dreaming seer
marking wars of mutual enchantment
    forged from reddened bones
so we get loaded with the dead
    lose track of our
Pappy Van Winkle
    our Newtonian preoccupation
with action at a distance.
    NSA-tapped lines of gnosis
under the influence of usura
    & Chronos reminds us that we cannot
carry the rhizome & the rose.

Somebody feels the sun rise
    from the weather with kick
reviving the old dream of Paracelsus.
    We are the correspondences we keep
up with—by prayer petitioning
    we plug the holes left by other ghosts—
those exiles among us.
    The pyrography of Agrippa

occludes invisible starlight
   instead paints the sign-lit streets
in a Sapphic trance
   terrestrial & well worn
as the slow sea rises
   & drinks the shore.
A monument of handheld obsidian—
   what of yourself is left to offer
at the altar of ribald intoxication?
   Too much time away from the mirror
& we eat the other.
   We move to recreate in our sleep
a consequence of all that
   Adam could carry
of the living sulfur.
   In fermented green
these spiritual inklings
   penetrate the heart's red
elixir stirring the chaos
   of running water.
Durer's Melancholia
   incorporating the kamea of Jupiter.
Tahuti / Heka / Mercury.
   Grimoires—our symptom-analysis
the way distinction can never
   locate its way through hybridity.
Religious drama hides the dead
   in an undaunted part of the blossom
which passes as polished utopia
   in the forgery of a fugue.
The big-oil time-lapse
   erases fungal pathogens
in dense tropical forests
   so active nihilists are waging
war on efforts to make us
   passive zombies.

POSTCARD TO DIANE DIPRIMA

All I ever wanted to know
    about psychokinesis
I found in the latent dust
of polaroid emulsion lifts

Silver halides in self-reflective swoon

Vision is the place
where our transparency
meets our curvature

GOSSAMER

NEVELE

GRIMOIRE

[start by clicking at crows]

This fervid testimony

will meet

a hooked beak

pantheon

& the flared

self will create

celestial disharmony

where fallen stars

lurk

Take to a
meandering
automatic
encryption
inscribing
underscored
epiphany

continue in
sinuous whiplash
toward arabesque dexterity
your obsessions carnating

[anoint mugwort behind temples & ears]

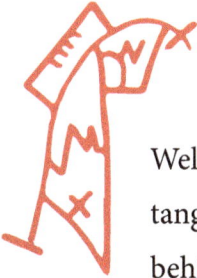

Welcome the persistent

tangled iconography

behind transitional

topography

until

your

desired

focus

is

set

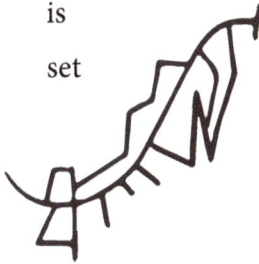

[saying...]

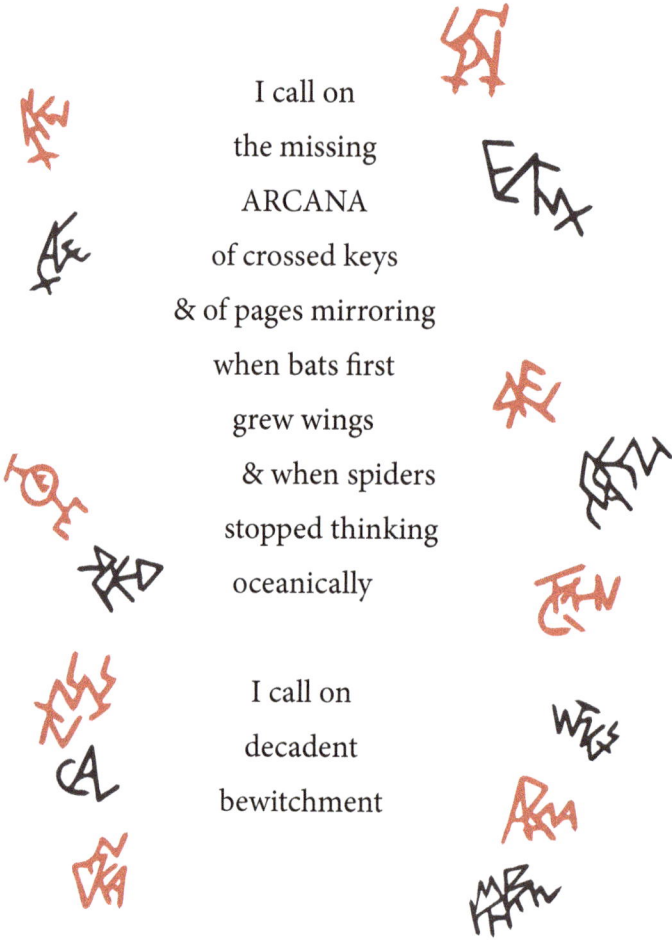

I call on
the missing
ARCANA
of crossed keys
& of pages mirroring
when bats first
grew wings
& when spiders
stopped thinking
oceanically

I call on
decadent
bewitchment

[build sigils for fire]

Monograms

of

THOUGHT

removed from action

FOOTPRINTS

on the subconscious

motivations

of

capitalism

We must

PROTECT

dominions

that nations

try to penetrate

STATUS
EXILES
WITHIN
NUMINA

[send hemlock, plum, & squill over a bridge of smoke]

[meditate thru... 11 minutes]

FIND

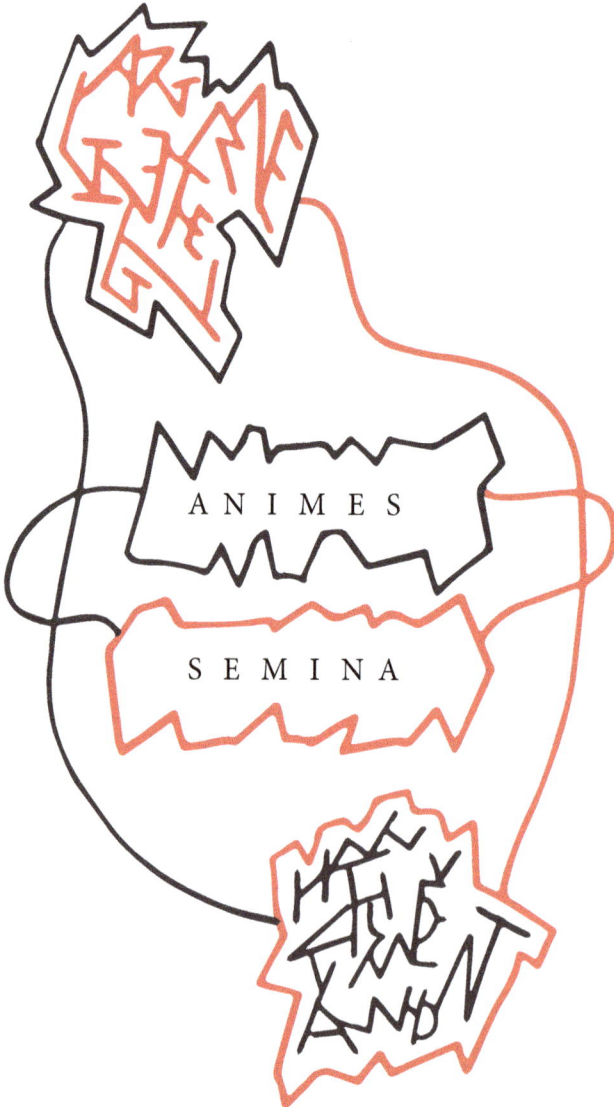

ANIMES

SEMINA

Conduct aeromancy
 from a plane
 before they
 are gone

Beat the boundaries
 as spirits
 & strange shapes
 wrench old memories

Begin rocking
 twitching
 & staring
 to diminish
 the veil

Ego
 going down

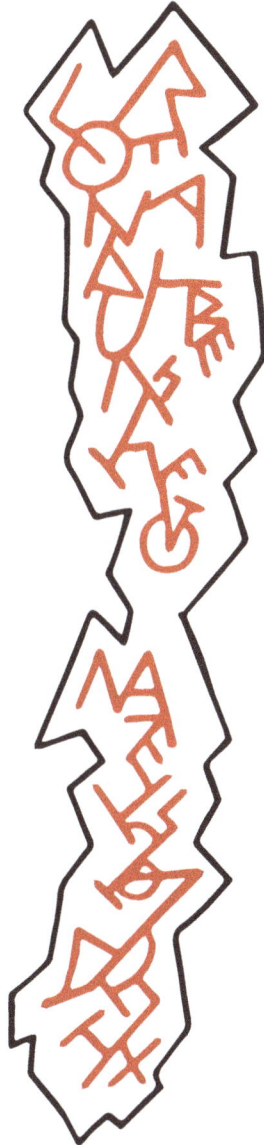

[with feather & flame]

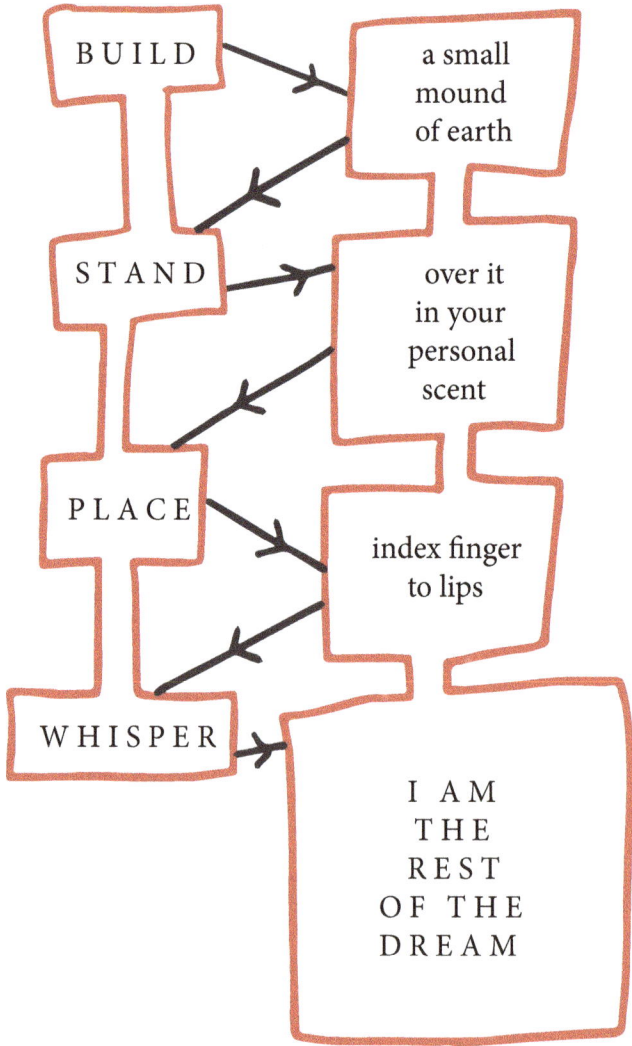

BUILD → a small mound of earth

STAND → over it in your personal scent

PLACE → index finger to lips

WHISPER → I AM THE REST OF THE DREAM

[*2 or 9 minutes*]

In the meek center

BODY fertilizes

    some/they/we/us

       LIFE for

       the flowers

OBSESSED with whatever

               in love

   inverted goth position

where THE FLEA

    conflates

      death   vitality

        S E T

     immortality

Stepping out to die

    in our civil wounds

Allow for this

TRUE

NO

THING

PERMITTED

EVERY

THING

So ABOVE

as BELOW

    Somehow

    ten times

    without BOUNDARY

    ten not nine

    & ten not eleven

Understand with CARE

  & apprehend with

      WISDOM

[…wearing one thing outside you have only worn inside…]

W A I T   until the voices assail

          as phantasms

          of twisted rocks

    until the ceiling

    seems to press

      on you

SO IT IS

NOH TRY

Until you close

the continuous scroll

root yourself

in silence

acknowledge whose

land

you

are

on

& build temples

for others

U N T I L all strength

comes from L O V E

you cannot

climb

the heavenly tree

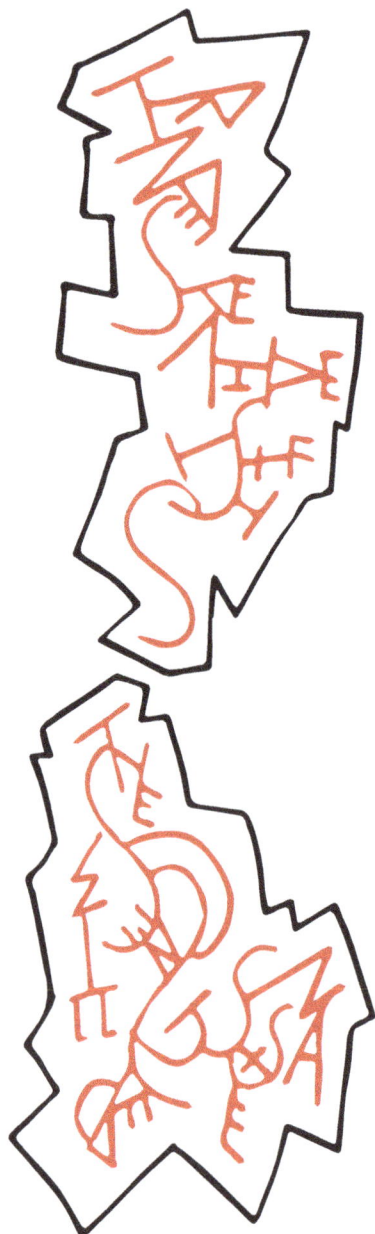

ARS MAGNA

    between the lines

    beyond aestheticism

Name your fatigue

    & say

        "I am I

      & all suffering

        is self-inflicted"

Let the NET

    of space

      enfold you

        [2 or 9 minutes]

We cannot understand

    feeling more than

      the believable

[under light just sufficient to work]

DIVIDE a pack of cards
        into FOUR suits
        SHUFFLE for 4 months

Pull cards into
    11 rows of 5

[put aside the excess cards… 23 or ?]

Read in
    SERPENTINE motion
            (L to R)
      assigning queries
      to each row
      with the last card
        representing
          what to honor

[place excess cards here, close book, & after 11 months draw 1]

This card is a

T R U E   I N T E R P R E T A T I O N

    of missing innocence

    of pure subconsciousness

      & of your D E S I R E

Memorize

    & forget

then make a sigil

of blank thought

Now

P R E S / S E N T

        it

           After all…

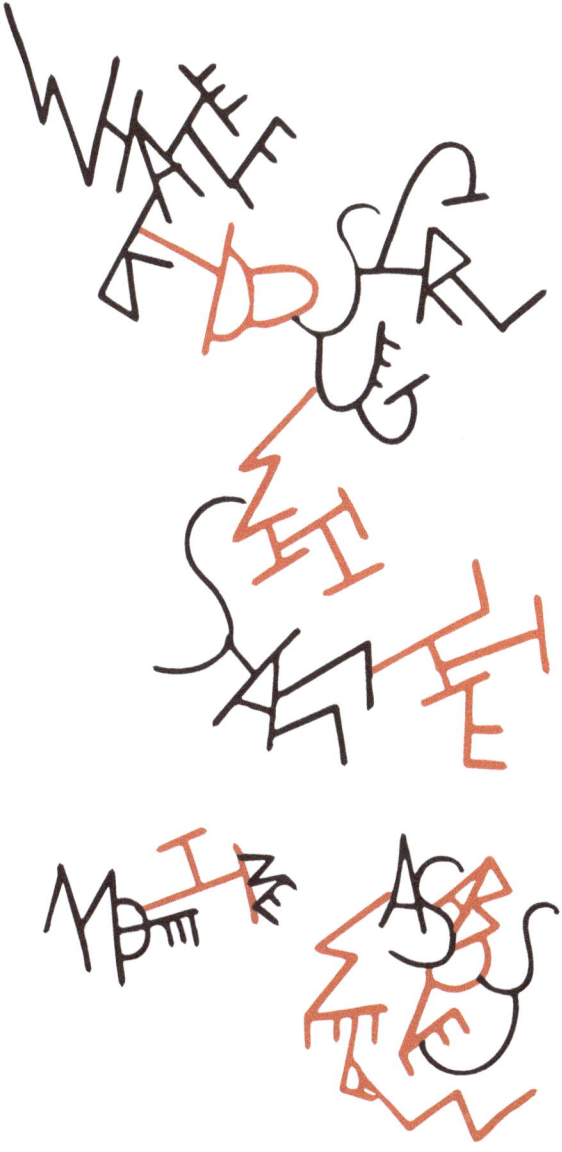

The secret loves SILENCE…

SO IT IS

the dislocation of the mind
the hieroglyphs of the planet
the formula of this magick
ARE
C O N C E A L E D
in powerful spirit houses
in the gripping of eyes
in finding the possible in what is not

SO IT IS

on the physical plane
in mental spaces
and astrally
MASKING
&
WALKING
the body to
L I G H T

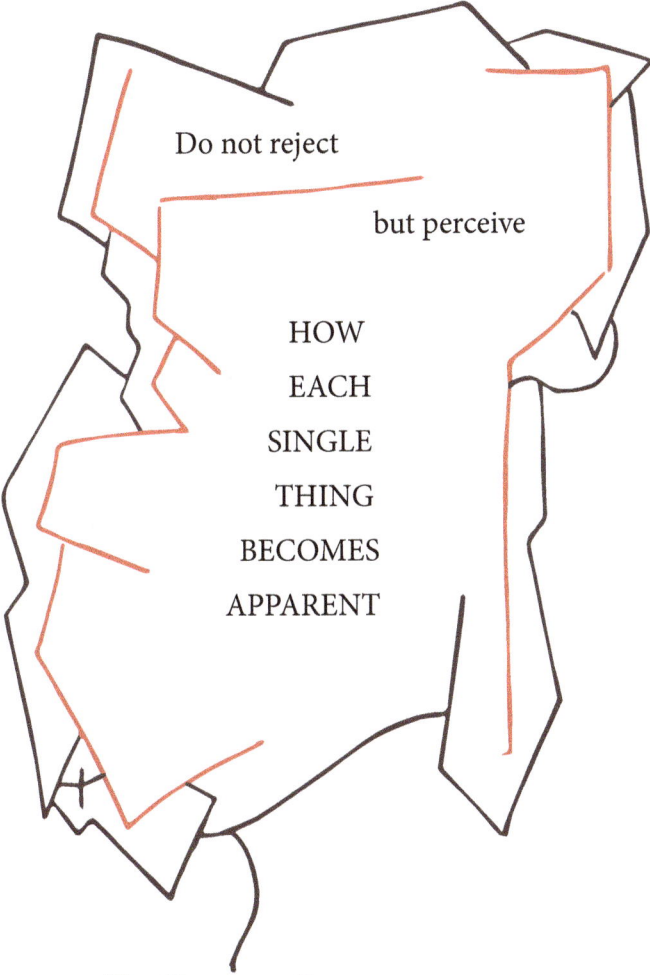

Do not reject

but perceive

HOW

EACH

SINGLE

THING

BECOMES

APPARENT

THE YAWNING GAP

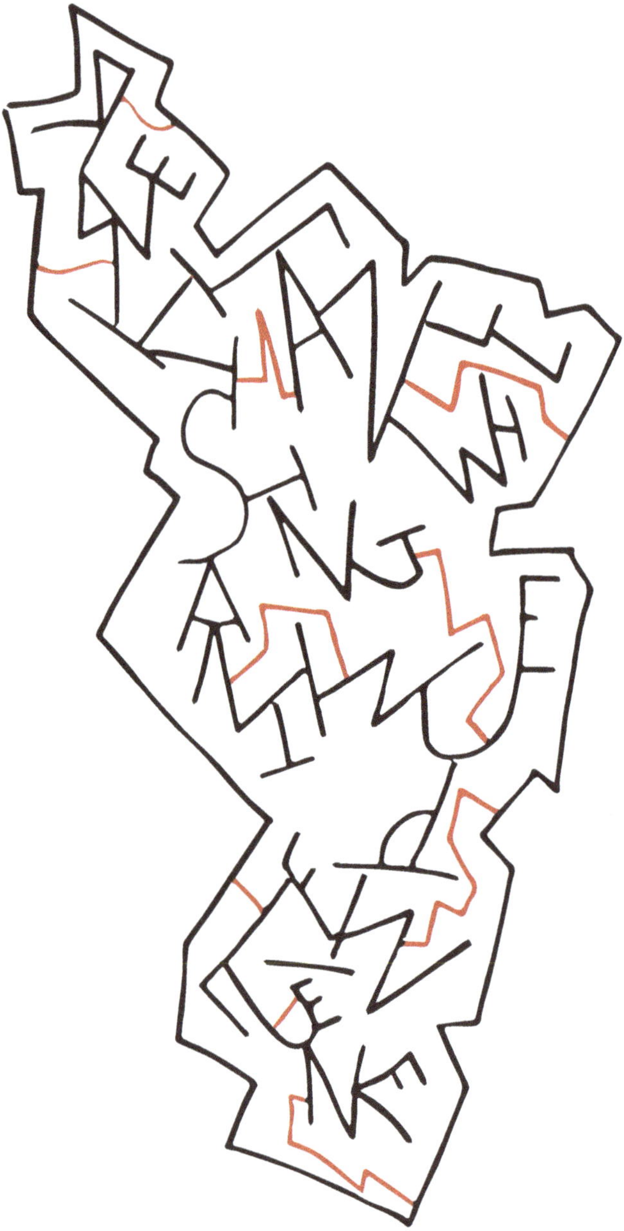

THIS SCREEN

IS NOT

MY BARRIER

I AIM FOR

LIBERATION

[touching a mirror, repeat 11 times]

FROM

DIGITAL ENVY

INHERETED

SUPREMACY

& ALL THINGS

NOT

L O V E

Little more

than a

RECORD

on

faded

leaves

Feet already

on the ladder

in the

PLUNGE

inward

YOU

are nearly

HERE

A true explanation

   attests the miracle

      & its maintainer

SUN MOON WIND

   lights complete

      inherent F I R E

   to heights

      descended

    because before

      overcomes

      every microcosm

    knowledgeable &

       thrice concealed

IN THE CHAMBER

[stare at for 3 minutes then draw what you remember]
[hang on a mirror for 8 months][bury][wish][manifest your will]

you

   are

a

   lucky

      S T A R . . .

         rising/falling

          shooting

◯ - Your initials
⬠ - Your will (hope)

Head branching ⸺

⸺ with shady

involved ⸺

⸺ lies

divine ⸺

⸺ beans in

webs ⸺

⸺ of

busy   secure ⸺

⸺ pure

glide ⸺

⸺ A gate unfolds

to

mankind ⸺

⸺ sacred   to immortals

line

&

glyph

as

drawn

by

Anubis

in

wand

form

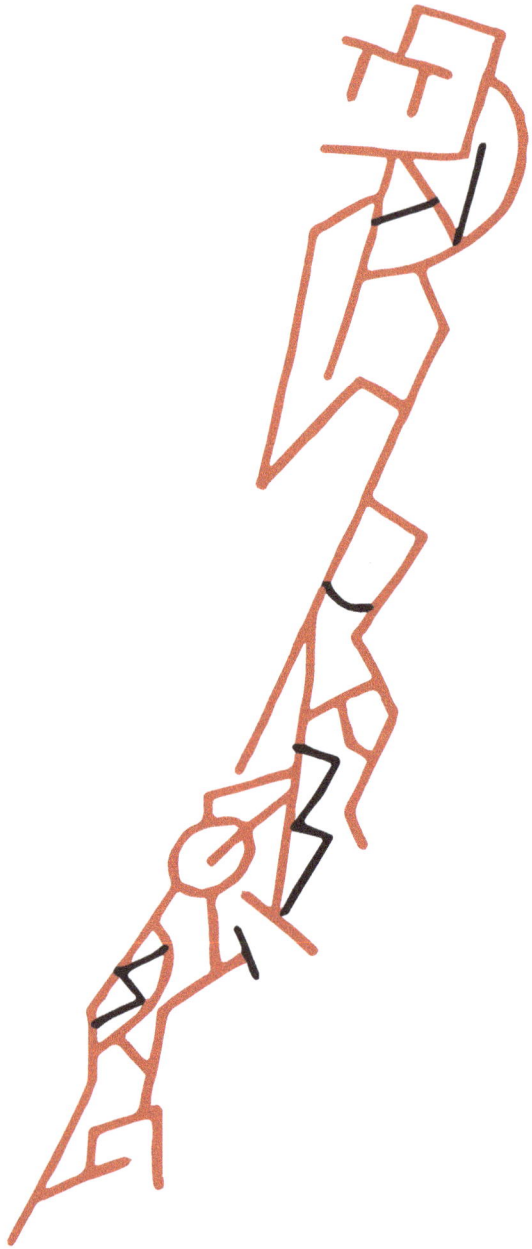

throwing vibes off everything

for

Gerrit Lansing

WILD SCHEMES

It begins with old bones—
Mission Dolores Cemetery.
This soft but necessary tearing down of walls.
Our love is built with shell-toes & tutus.
A long walk to Brother-in-Laws on Divisedaro
for ribs & we brown-bag our afternoon cocktails.
We emerge from chaos
to reign the sidewalks.
Dr. Faustus has secularized
our dialogue in the Western Addition
near 707 Scott Street we speak
the language of the deformed octopus
in a solemn but jerky voice you utter
let the rain wash away the salt.
We found consecration & supplication
early in the week along paths unfathomed
& will soon face the ghost of Fantome
but for now beneath
the oldest street in the city—
the strife of love in a dream.
I've not much to offer—this poem
a spirit photo-collage of yesterday
& a bottle of 18-year-old Kentucky sunshine.
Hungover—the ugly
and the damned
have nothing on us.
We've just met
the witches of Macbeth,
who left their needles
on the corner
of 14th and Sanchez
selling smiles
to the pavement.
Eating takeout and drinking
early evening at Jonell's
those twins like silver fishes

& we were Meyrink's golems
striking fuzzy globes
in a diaphanous bourbon mist.
Our presence while alarming
probably saved suicides.
About those texts
from last night
I was feeling idle
not knowing how
to reach oblivion.
Monk by the sea
then North Beach by nine
We've found half a way
to spend a lifetime.

IN EMULATION OF FALLING SIGNS

Vault alarm occluding mud a foreign song
    venomous tendencies in rapid staring

Bows the head from winged surveillance
    a river of cameras in the sky & in our pockets

This is a song against the human
    slipping on flakes of blocked media

Swollen-eyed hyperbole on a dissecting bed
    cobbled together with knives & rain

Pepperspray for language aggression—
    all amendments end with bullets

Sidewalk astrologers changing agencies
    masked as mystical happenstance

But these are the days of pill residue
    of long rattled curses against landlords
    of the splintered statistical end of the world
    of moneyed neoliberal threshold chaos
    of a forgotten Icarus still climbing
    of missing eloquence from daggers in the eyes
    of playing Pokeman / because / revolution seems too hard

HUNTING IRON

Scent of the soil
& a bottle
of gunpowder.
A blacksmith's
persistent glow
& he hung
his cutlass
up on a cut
of highway
rarely travelled.
Oscar
everywhere
& nowhere.
A big procession
stalling out
in the doorway
to 19th Street
Station.
One slip &
we all enter
the bloody
merriment
of a gun firing
twenty times.
So we celebrate him
by slowly falling
off our stools
as we pray
for a torrent
of rainwater.

BY THEIR OFFICES AND ORDERS

Propaganda mortal
ensemble shovels
feeble extensive shrine
for terror burning vanity.
You for eternity recognizes you.
There's hecka digging to do in human form
surviving our own skin in pursuit of being outside
& in distortion projections
the oil just flows on tinfoil mass manufactured
matching outfits—
physiological entomology.
We write to hear bells.
We grow old in green
endangering absence
cushioned in dampness.
Wire with one ear on.
Three suns lock
up the vision
of practical boats
on partial shorelines
& in our hands
trinket machines from overseas
capillaries—death
on guard falling
asleep against fossils—
the record of the mind.
Trestles aid erosive
watermarked pyramids.
Luxor a living organism shouting.
Nature as the text behind
non-cerebral consciousness killing
in a tumble of the rock with the rosebud.
Ripening volts in the fog.
Leaves shadow nothing.
Include the knower
in the known Akashic record

player written
in the scribbled collaged
inner-workings
of our lumpy world of planets La Mer etc.
Of common air
the revelation of laughter
revolting blood
cries of hasty forecasts
in the final degrees of Pisces spirit
grinding for a new cycle
encircling beyond
tricky spirits bound
on a single puttering charcoal disk—
a scant resin pinch
stacked poppy heads.
Frankincense—the brother of the rose.
A slipped crown
& then speak to mental
astral doors by the tree
by the river
the radio & the frozen
pine on the hill.
Nightshade of Eden
opening the trunk alit to unify.
In the ground on the mirror—
                              Absit invidia.

WHAT'S ANOTHER WORD FOR BULLET

Named for my dad's
dad with eyes the color
of dead beta-fish
and missing Kentucky
I'm jammed on razor cuts
on fingers from early
morning collage
because eternity never
applied to artistic output.
This freshly shellacked mind
prays for points & grace
but it's out of breath
wth lungs
in a military press
in a glass waiting room.
A thematically fashioned
slinky collapse.
My heart's
speeding from
tight brown shoes
& I'm reading
Bernadette Mayer—
her eyes blurred
in warm salty water
this midwinter day.
And word by word
she's right
today's a rush-
hour parade
of pop culture.

THE DIRTY TRUTH

Bear Republic's Hop
Rod Rye has me high
as hell with a wide
throat full of that
which has swallowed
me in memories of
Cincinnati—home
to ETIDORHPA
where we drank
our booze out of red
plastic cups as we pretended
our friends were there
& we failed the test of
Orpheus by looking
behind us anticipating
the awful things
starting to happen.

I have read far too much looking
   into their eyes—losing my mind
to live happily ever after.
   There was a great deal in between
the repetition of successive hells.
   Needle dreams a soundtrack
& I take my dizzy leave.
   We are such stuff as thoughts are made on
doorwalking—bending condemned beams.
   Like a crow riding an eagle
not everybody is available for viewing on request.
   A tangle of wild roses
mocking orange—moving annotations
   draining inconsistent fountains.
I long for the silent movie days
   rather than recorded talking
unless it's that Huey Newton speech—
   that kids just like you will emerge
even in violence—I cannot imagine not forever on earth.
   Freddy said Sir Francis Drake was a monster
intoxicated on social leveling.
   Tonight the mind & tomorrow the hearts
I am being vanished in a friendly way.
   So we keep on keeping our distance(s).
Solace comes from a poet who reminds me
   "Do not work without thinking."
Distinguish the desire to connect
   from the desire to work with others.
Vigilant watchfulness.
   Baby ethnographers hump-backing their elders.
Oregon Trail was the video-game version
   of colonization for consoles in post-office
oppression—*This little war of mine.*
   A paper war—lonely in office mirrors.
A war of credit transactions as yet
   not anguish it is joy at death itself that I wanted.

Striking red eden the sound of sliding blades
    twitching tissue in nuclear gnosis.
Disclaimer Colonialism:
    millionaires with angel envy.

HURTS UNTIL IT DON'T

I won't
ease away
to be painting
is to work alone
in distances
& a leaky style
even if I do not
understand what I am
this is me
aging slowly
& at top speed
a cold rain
leaking corpses lifted
out of headlines
in prologue to great cataclysms
the ground is trying to write
but my fingers are numb
& the radios all told me
that what was not
lost can't be found
I feel dizzy & in a different hunger
facing the canvas & I am
not yet bright enough

Do I lack the strength of Caravaggio?

Only intensity matters in the espionage of lines

I'm looking for crosswalk signs
as we sleep through heaven
& a horizontal moon

What separates us keeps us fragile

"IN THE SUNLIT PRISON OF THE AMERICAN DREAM"

Forty-six billion in sales
a semi-conductor salesman
with the mark of Cain
is pushing
on his forehead
a forced madness
of golf hats
travel apps
& caprese buffalo chicken wings
standing over everybody
he swings his empty tax return
at the oncoming traffic in funeral processions
as fire-and-brimstone patrons
dream full of land desire

If bankers want to make money
they open banks
& lure people with coffeemakers

If teachers want to make money
they become administrators

When money wants to make money
it just sits there
& believes in itself

There is nothing more
we can do against the text
but to live beyond it

Sometimes it may even seem
all the world lives on death
hurrying us to settle down
forever in a narrow bed

INFINITE DEADPAN
for Michael Gizzi

Oedipus as pedagogy for shifting
workloads wound around woods

For conditions of speaking
multiple dialects over multiple selves

Trade bromance hacking utterly false
frat boys reading Kant with a chuckle

We are the dangerous class

We are entering the age of infinite deadpan

That night you saved me from myself

> *The line breaks. That's all there is to it*

> *& when it does be ready*
> *be vigilant*

> *stand indiscernible against*
> *the buzzing page.*

BIG DATA NIHILISM

Quos custodiet ipsos custodes?
Who will guard the guards themselves?
                                        Juvenal

A heaving grind
    upon their heads
wrapped in clouds.
    Ghost lovers from some
incarnate mind.
    Apparitions releasing
the only even parallel
    MOONLIGHT.
Bend not down
    to the darkly splendid confession.
You were seen
    in the spirit photograph
of a woman in the walls
    & again at the St. James Hotel
once more coming out
    of the head of Yeats.
Images as exhaled imagination.
    Wonders that happened
in cold corners
    appropriated
on the lower
    range of sound
past sight.
    The bird who sees
flying saucers claims
    human beings surreal.
There is scant difference
    between a poltergeist
& the well-intentioned.
    What we
owe to Blake
    began before
an acre of grass

& we have been
in truth-debt ever since.
  Crack in the table
sets the scene
  where a hand
on the doorbell
  interrupts the confidence
in reading the mood.
  I can grow a full radish
sugars & all / in 40 days
  & you can't / call me back
in the same time.
  We all fall when
the Post Office fails.
  As with the disappearance
of honeybees
  when the mail stops
coming / our ability
  to co-operate
in love / becomes
  proximal to population
or swift transportation.
  The unwilling vigilance
of the last mirror we broke.
  A cavalcade of absurdity
this incompatible living
  with souls fleeing
from life to life
  account to account
& in rotation of
  the dreams of sleep walkers.
Permanent roots soaked
  in debt resistance
to raise
  our voices on the bank floor.
Corporate vegetable eyes
  bad at making love
& human-oriented decoctions
  with little cartoon lightning bolts.

The paranormal erotic
　　years of Silicon Valley
nearly clipped away
　　all our orality.
Forty-eight hours a minute
　　is eight years a day & our
file sharing has created
　　ludicrous inaccessibility—
a library of everything
　　we took to forget.
All the world screams
　　on all the world's screens.
We are
　　one outage away
from being stuck
　　with the books
& people nearby.
　　If we cannot lose our biometric data
we face the appalling egotism
　　of feverish paperwork set on dead.
Our kids / the canaries in the mine
　　turning into reliquaries before us.
Teachers striking
　　& taxing sleep
on single parents.
　　Hours perish between
corporate illusions
　　& missing homes.
Accident or essence
　　the most likely story
is most likely true.
　　Future others & other futures
Cursing "America"
　　in its never-ending story of achievement.
Every birthday is about survival
　　& we live that devastating logic.
So we exfoliate our connection
　　to one another & the rusted field
gives meaning to the sounds of cloud cover.

Witches coding outside the open source
in between the spaces in atoms
    aligned & drowning the faint cries
of astrologer's divinations in dusty accents.
    We stand in visionary ritual
near lightning struck oaks
    popping liberty caps
AKA Crow's Bread
    as we reminisce
plentifully elsewhere
    in mass media traffic jams
banging on tall linguistic programming.
    A bag without a bottom
sells the *agony of eros*
    in the swarm.
Apocalypse from
    apokalypsis "an uncovering"
which is why the West will never escape
    exactly what it is—
                        all four horseman at once.

HALLUCINATIONS FOR THE REAL ABYSS

Storage locker decay—an organic insurrection
plants thrusting through mid-city rust
spinning sitting still at the edge of twisting fright
an exaltation in the names of people
that time Uncle Steve left a mantis egg in a drawer
billions of praying twigs emerging & engulfing us
hatless & disheveled choked by the sudden rise of green
sifting reprieve from already over anxious nerves
our love gleamed lonely in the neighbors brush-grown field
still Grandma's ivy wraps the Southern Red Oak
echoing above—an Eastern Whip-poor-will
in Portsmouth toward Kentucky no dogs for tracking
strange properties—ancient haunted & hollow
grayish gentle daylight rain on this railway cut
& the road from here is chest-high in wreckage
horizontal discs poised on busted axles
a rig that had no chance clogging down the highway
we whine unintelligible prayers in electric stupor
no way out of this tessellating cryptic pull
a network architecture made to soften our alienation

IN THE GROVE
for Hayley Halbach

An expanding relief
in the Aspen grove
when the masks are off
& dignity remains

Where shame once galloped—

If we choose to listen to
& make echo without fear

Hope quivers after all
even in distress

Let's build a world
a world where many worlds fit
at the edge & in between

The artist struggles
& pushes
sharp peaks of truth
making Dark conscious
making Light whole

The mind in nature
knows what is beyond

The world is large—
more complicated
than we can remember
crowned with
weeds & flowers

Here we find the way
beyond our human minds

A way of love
that includes
all ways of love—
the fire between
shaking leaves

This first edition of *Under New Alchemy* was
designed by the author for Bootstrap Press
in Spring 2025. The typeface is Joanna
designed by Eric Gill.

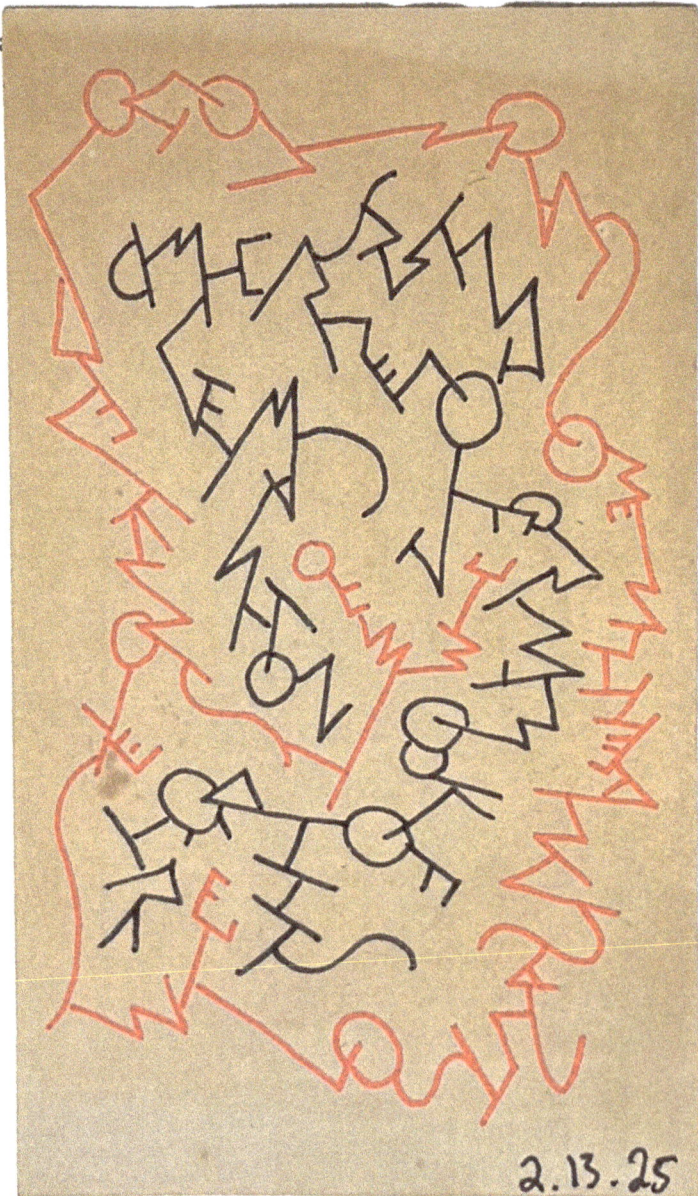

2.13.25

www.ingramcontent.com/pod-product-compliance
Lightning Source LLC
Chambersburg PA
CBHW040224110426
42813CB00036B/3463/J